10
Traits
of
Winning Athletes

George Mangum

PublishAmerica
Baltimore

PublishAmerica has allowed this work to remain exactly as the author intended, verbatim, without editorial input.

Hardcover 978-1-4512-9964-9
Softcover 978-1-4489-4097-4
PUBLISHED BY PUBLISHAMERICA, LLLP
www.publishamerica.com
Baltimore

Printed in the United States of America

Contents

About Me

Okay, my name is George Mangum, and I have been involved in sports for most of my life.

My sports obsession (no, really, an obsession) began in 1967. I always played sports, but I became a fan after my dad introduced me to the San Francisco Giants and the Oakland Raiders. I watched them on one of those floor model, kinda color televisions; the kind which had no cable, no satellite, or no remote. Life was tough.

I continued competing in sports, playing baseball all the way through college and attending free-agent tryouts, but decided to get on with a career. I started teaching P.E. in 1985 in the High Desert of California (a community in between Los Angeles and Las Vegas). During this time, I developed my coaching skills and have recently developed Ath-Elites, a sports performance training company for athletes from twelve years old to the professional level. The training methodology that I use is for one purpose only, *to prepare athletes to win.* My athletes do not hear about being competitive or just doing the best job possible. If I did that, I would be untrue to those who have been entrusted to me.

Now, during all of these years, I always studied the winning and losing dynamics of sports. I made notes of my observations throughout the years. I always wondered about how some players with the same talent level would win more consistently their competitors. There was something that they were or something that they did which separated them, and that is what *10 Traits of Winning Athletes* is all about.

I've spoken with sports psychologists and read some of their writings, yet they do not seem to get what winning is about. I heard a lot about goal setting and success, but little about winning. There are countless athletes who are "great" and many who have had successful careers. I am not denying that. However, this book focuses on winning, which is separate from success and greatness.

Consequently, when I watch sports, I now focus on those things that winning players and winning teams do. I watch how winning takes place or does not. There are some definite things that occur that separate winners from players (did you get that? winners vs. players?), and the *10 Traits* explains these things.

About the Book

These are random thoughts about the book which I think you should know before reading it.

1. The Purpose: The primary reason for the *10 Traits* is to outline why winning athletes win. There are many more traits; however, these are ten important ones. That's why I did not call it *The 10 Traits...*, get it? Heck, if you want to make up some more, that's totally okay.

2. The Content: All right, I admit it! I want the book to be highly regarded as far as its literary content, but that may not happen. Oh, don't get me wrong, the material is true and it is designed to be read easily, but my skill-set may not be with the pen. However, those who read it will be impacted and it should help those who want to transform from players/ competitors to winners. I definitely use the K.I.S.S. method (Keep It Short and Sweet).

3. The Style: I have a style and I cannot deny it. The book needs to be straight-forward and easy to read. If I try to impress anybody, I won't because it won't be me. Consequently, the information is what needs to be said, and you have to decide what you will do with it.

4. The Impact: If you are an athlete, you will be able to incorporate some or all of these ten traits. If and when you do, your transformation from player to winner will begin.

5. Disclaimer: Let's get this out of the way. Very rarely will I use the word loser. I am not one of those authors who write negative things about others. There has to be a good reason for calling someone a loser, and athletics is not one of them. If anybody reading this feels like if they do not meet any of these ten traits that they are a loser, that's on you. I do not have a definition for the word

loser. I am way more concerned about winning and winners than I am about losing.

6.   Format: Each section will include an opening explanation, where I try to explain myself. Next, there will be a focus athlete, someone who is winning in this current era. After that, there will be a memorable moment of an athlete whose winning efforts can be related to this book. Finally, I will recount a story of athletes whom I have coached or observed and who have won at their level, proving that winning takes place at all levels. These ending stories are about winning, and do not necessarily match-up with the topic being discussed.

Research Information

It is important to know that I have held on to this information for a year. What that means is that I wrote the book, then waited a full year to observe if what I originally said was correct or not. I first completed the book in January 2009 and I will have it finalized in January 2010.

The information presented is based on the criteria of observation of athletes, interaction with athletes, participation in athletics, and daily research of athletics.

I am proud to say that most of what I wrote stood the test of time over the past year. I will add that I looked at my information critically. There were some changes throughout the year because of how things played out and I made them. That means that several athletes were originally a focus of the book, but were removed after having observed them for a full year. This way, I would feel true to myself and the readers by submitting material which passed my own tough requirements, and it does.

The reality is that I did not want to write a book that was thrown together recklessly. The *10 Traits* has been twenty-five years in the making and waiting one more year to satisfy my "commitment of integrity" was totally worth it.

Acknowledgement

I couldn't believe it. On Saturday, January 30, 2010, I was sitting here, fretting about the legitimacy of my book and its contents. I have to be honest. I know what I'm talking about and have no doubts about my presentation or motivation for writing this. I have taught this stuff to athletes, corporations, and anybody else who might listen, but, I needed something that would solidify what it was I was saying. Some of the information presented here has never been heard by so many who need to hear it, and I want to make sure that *10 Traits* will hold up to the test of the readers. Then, in an instant, I had my own personal **"Dickie V. moment"**. Later in the book, I talk about the now supernatural Jeter Moment, but my own encounter with this new Dickie V. phenomenon convinced me I was right in what I was doing.

I turned on the tube to watch some college hoops, and watched a little of the Kansas—Kansas State basketball game. At the same time, I was checking out some of the latest football recruiting news online, when one of the Kansas players made a basket to put them into the lead. Much to my utter, much needed shock, legendary basketball announcer Dick Vitale (aka Dickie V.) called the player a winner (Sherron Collins I think), then confirmed some of the things I have written in book. After having referred to Collins as a winner, he also mentioned that Peyton Manning, Derek Jeter, and Tim Tebow were winners as well. Bro, he didn't say great players or superstars, or even "Diaper Dandies;" he said winners.

Now, this may not seem like a big deal to anybody else, but it was huge for me. Vitale, who has no idea who I am, confirmed everything that I believe, and said it to a national audience. He talked about winners, and just happened to mention athletes I have listed in the book. Upon hearing that, I had what my daughters call "a big fat Silva," a feeling of momentary, self-willed feeling of superiority (I think). I was dancing around the room, recreating the original boxing sequence from the movie, *Rocky*.

Throughout the book, you will read about winning, and how it is different than success and greatness. Dick Vitale and I, apparently, have the same notion of who winners are and who winners are not. I can live that (and have another "big fat Silva," if only for a moment).

Dickie V., Sir Richard, Mr. Vitale (whatever), thank you for your amazing ability to spot winners. Call me, and we'll do lunch (your treat).

Trait 1

Winners are Convinced

Win-Definition: Convinced—A fact, not a belief.

Explanation: News alert. Goals and dreams are weak. Destinations are what winners have. Too many people end up in life with goals and dreams, yet little accomplishment. However, winners decide what they will do and accomplish what they have decided to do. Well, winning athletes are the same. Hey, winners have a destination to win, not hope or dream to win. There is no alternative that even registers. This destination is so clear that they are convinced that they deserve to win and that they will win. Did you catch that? They are convinced that they will win, not should win, can win, or might win. Man, everybody **should** win, but winners are convinced that they **will** win. To explain this further, winners don't believe that they will win, they know they will win. Do you have a destination to win or goal to win? You choose (winners already have).

Focus Athlete: If you watch the National Basketball Association (NBA), the world witnessed an athlete who had a destination to win. Kobe Bryant, before the 2009 NBA playoffs even began, had already decided that he and the Los Angeles Lakers would win. He was convinced that the Lakers would win and deserved to win. Since I live in SoCal, I don't think anybody here thought any differently about this either. There was no way they were going to lose this series, and Kobe made sure of that.

Looking back, you can say that LeBron James of the Cleveland Cavaliers had a goal to win, as did Dwight Howard of the Orlando Magic. But, and I am talking about a "big but," Kobe's heart was set on this and nothing short of a catastrophic injury was going to change that. There was no other outcome for Kobe but winning. Nothing else was considered. I really think that if Kobe's leg would have just kinda fallen off, he would have just hopped his way to a win.

Kobe is convinced that he will win. It's fact, not belief. It's his destination, not his goal or dream.

Memorable Moment: A memorable moment occurred shortly after I began the book. I watched this year's football game between the University of Southern California (USC) and Ohio State University (OSU), one that ended very closely. USC's freshman quarterback Matt Barkley guided the Trojans to a winning touchdown drive as game was coming to an end. Barkley had not had a great game up to that point. He suffered an injury and was facing more than 100,000 OSU fans who were screaming their brains out, trying to keep Barkley from doing his thing. Needless to say, USC won the game, and Barkley had this to say when being interviewed afterwards. When asked about the last minute winning touchdown drive, Barkley kind of just said, "We're Trojans. That's what we do."

Man oh man. Matt Barkley, aged nineteen at the time, was convinced that the Trojans would win because that is what USC football teams do. They win. You see, Barkley had gone beyond believing that they would win. He knew they would win. It was simply a fact, much like two plus two equals four.

Now, I know that the Trojans did not have the season he was planning for, but ended up with a win at the 2009 Emerald Bowl. But, you have to know that Barkley already had winning in his heart. He is convinced that he and his team will win every time they take the field. Anything else is not considered.

"That's Winning" Personal Story: Several years ago, I spoke with a young man named Josh who received scholarship offers to play quarterback for several colleges. The one he chose already had an all-league quarterback playing. I asked him why he chose that school instead of one where he could probably play immediately. He said that this was the school he felt best about going to and it offered what he wanted academically. Again, I questioned him about playing time at quarterback. What he said next floored me.

At just seventeen years old, he simply said that he would just "outwork and outperform" the other quarterback until he got the position. No goals, no dreams, just winning. Wouldn't you know it? He got the position by the fourth game and stayed there until he graduated, leading his team to winning records each of his years there. He translated his destination to win by finishing law school and starting his own practice. Don't you love winning?

Trait 2

Winners are Captains

Win-Definition: Captains—Those who not only lead others, but cause them to change into winners themselves.

Explanation: Captains are more than the leaders of their groups, their ships, their teams. Captains, because of who they are, cause people to change. They don't necessarily even have to say anything and they certainly do not have to have the title of captain. Yet, because they are winners, they cause those around them to change into the winners that they are. Have you ever seen a team of talented athletes who couldn't win because there was no captain? We all have, too many times. Come on, the only people who don't want winners on their teams are the ones who either don't want to win or the ones who do not to be shown-up because they are not winners. Leadership has become a cheapened term these days. However, being a captain means that a person is someone who gets others to win, actively or by example. Whereas leadership is about influence, which anyone can do, captainship is about winning, which many don't do.

Focus Athlete: All I know is this. If you play on the same team as legendary National Football League (NFL) quarterback Brett Favre, you will become a winner. It seems that whatever team Favre plays on, they begin to win, and the players become winners. I don't know what it is, but winning and Favre probably have the same definition in the dictionary.

The first bit of evidence is that those around Favre begin playing better almost immediately. It doesn't matter if it is the Green Bay Packers or the New York Jets, the teams begin to win. The Minnesota Vikings are winning this year, largely because Favre is their quarterback.

Favre causes those around him to become winners. I don't think that Favre needs the title of captain and I don't think Favre does a whole lot of yelling at his teammates. They just start winning, which points to Favre's role as a winner/ captain.

Memorable Moment: It was professional baseball's 2001 American League Championship Series (ALCS) between the Oakland A's and the New York Yankees. These are the times when winners are shown to be who they really are, and this one is no different. The captain here is a pure winner, the Yankees' Derek Jeter.

It was late in the game and Jeremy Giambi of the A's was speeding around third base and was certain to score the game's go-ahead run. The ball had been thrown towards the infield, about to bounce away harmlessly, until something happened that only a winner would do.

We all watched, assuming that Giambi would score. Suddenly, there's Jeter. Normally, a shortstop, Jeter's position, should never be as close to home plate as he was, but that doesn't matter. Almost supernaturally, Jeter sprinted toward the badly thrown ball, grabbed it with his bare hand, flipped it backwards to the catcher, and Giambi was tagged out, saving the day for the Yankees. It is now referred to as the "Jeter Moment." Now, all of this stuff happened before we could really comprehend what had just happened. Jeter, the Yankee captain, the winner who commands the Yankees' ship so to speak, did the miraculous, which of course, is pretty normal for him.

If you know anything about the Yankees, Jeter is the captain, and is compared to the immortal Babe Ruth. Because Jeter is a winner, the others on the Yankees become winners too, even if they come from another team. For crying out loud, he just captained them to the 2009 World Series championship over the Philadelphia Phillies. Without Jeter's captainship, who knows if the Yankees would have even made it to the World Series, much less win it.

Anybody can influence somebody else, but winners are captains whose actions, words, or performance cause those around them to become winners.

"That's Winning" Personal Story: Shannon was a women's volleyball player for a university located in Southern California. When she received her scholarship, the coach told her that she had a great chance to be named as a captain her freshman year. Her freshman year was almost disastrous, causing her to contemplate quitting and focusing on her studies. The worst part was that she had lost her starting position during the year, and lost the chance to be the captain that she really was. Up until that point, she had always won and was the captain of her teams. Teammates became winners by playing on the same teams with her. She was a winner and a captain, but this was testing her.

After the season and after reviewing the situation, she realized that she was a winner that the team needed, and that she was going to be the starting setter again. I asked her if this was her goal, and she said that it wasn't really a goal, it was just what she was going to do. So, during the summer, she did what she needed to do and regained the starting position and re-established herself as a captain. She put in the time to improve her game and organized team activities, not because of what she was told to do, but rather because of who she was, a winner.

By the end of the season, she had placed herself into the record books at the school and began immediately preparing for the next season. Her captainship has influenced those around her to become winners, which reflects the captain that she is.

Trait 3

Winners are Conditioned

Win-Definition: Conditioned—When a winner is physically prepared to defeat their opponent.
Prepared beyond the requirements.

Explanation: You gotta know as a PE teacher and the founder of Ath-Elites, we profess that conditioning is a foundation of winning athletes. And, you must know how we respond when we see poorly conditioned athletes. How can an athlete win if they cannot perform at a winning level longer or better than their opponent does? Winners invest in training, and too many times, athletes rely on talent, which only goes so far. In my information about Ath-Elites, I proclaim with confidence that, "Ath-Elites begins where genetics leave off," and "If you can't beat your opponent with talent, beat them with training." Hey, unless I've missed something, trying to change genetics is impossible. However, training is available to all those who are winners or those who have a destination to win.

Have you ever seen a more gifted athlete beaten by one who is better conditioned? Uh, it happens more than we would like to think. The classic case is in boxing. Mercy, if an athlete isn't conditioned here, it's possible that they could get their "bell seriously rung." And why in the world do we hear about professional athletes who get "gassed"? Winning athletes practice what I call the **Rule of Two.** They are prepared to go "two" further than their opponents, whether it is two feet, two quarters, or two games. There's no getting "gassed" when you're a winner. What is up with that? It had to be heartbreaking for the men's U.S. soccer team to admit losing a 2009 championship game to the Brazilian team due to a lack of conditioning.

As a note, why is it that when a prominent athlete has a poor season, they always seem to refocus on their conditioning to help them get back to winning?

Focus Athlete: The National Basketball Association (NBA) had their yearly draft of players, and the Los Angeles Clippers, using the first overall pick, drafted Blake Griffin, college basketball's top player, from the University of Oklahoma. Griffin's pro career has yet to start because of injuries, yet it doesn't change these facts.

If you never watched him play, he is freaking scary, combining power, agility, and stamina with the heart of a winner. Griffin became such a winning, dominant player because his training program is superior to most. In researching Griffin, it was reported that his coaches had to, literally, chase Griffin out of the weight room and the plyometrics area.

When they asked Griffin why he trained so hard, he stated that he did so in order to win. Bam, baby! Blake trains, or, excuse me, prepares to win through his conditioning program. Now, like most others, he could put in this time in order to be great or famous or successful, but noooooo, he does this amount of conditioning in order to win. How many others are using their talent only? How many others are not conditioning at all and are going to be too tired when they or the team really needs them? Well, when they face Blake Griffin, their talent is not going to be enough, I guarantee it.

Memorable Moment: Years ago, I was skimming through a magazine and I came to an ad by the shoe giant, Nike. In the tradition of Nike marketing's dramatic presentations, this one did not let us down as readers.

The picture showed a female athlete, bent over, sweating profusely, and completely exhausted. Across the bottom of the ad were the words, "This is her day off!" Oh man, did you just feel those goose bumps up and down your spine? That was so sweet. It totally told a story of what a winning athlete was all about. When everyone else spent their days off in other ways, this athlete was making sure that she continued to win.

Oh, and I think I should tell you this. That female athlete was none other than Women's National Basketball Association's (WNBA) superstar, Lisa Leslie, who has won at every level she has ever played at. And, don't kid yourself, bucko. Lisa Leslie is beatable if she just uses her talents and abilities. But, that is not the case here. Is anybody getting this? Lisa Leslie, the picture of athletic super stardom, works out, trains, and prepares to win when her competition is having ice cream. Ice cream or WNBA champion? Should I even have to suggest this?

"That's Winning" Personal Story: At the risk of hurting feelings, I still must tell this story. I worked with a young lady named Desiree, who was an all-league shortstop in softball her freshman year in high school, but she was too heavy for her own good. During that year, a college scout had already started noticing her, which probably did more harm than good. She assumed talent would carry her through, and that was all that she needed. By the time her junior year rolled around, she was heavier than ever and sitting on the bench, moaning about how the coach had begun to dislike her. I had to tell her that it wasn't her coach who had changed, but her performance had gone down because of her poor conditioning. The coach had to play another girl who was producing.

I told her this only once and left her alone, but it took her several more weeks to get the message. The season was winding down, and she came to me in tears. She told me her goal was to get her spot back at shortstop and to revive the interests of college scouts who had stopped contacting her. I stopped her right away and asked, "Is getting this position back a goal or a destination?" I had to explain that a goal would allow her to try hard, but maybe wouldn't be enough to get her the position back. I explained to her that if getting this position back became her destination, she would do what it took to "win" it back.

She began "preparing to win" immediately. On the days she did not want to prepare, she did anyway. By the time her senior softball season rolled around, she was in condition to win back her position, which she did easily. Now, after having gone to college on a softball scholarship, she became a softball coach and is a fanatic about her girls' fitness and conditioning. She told me, *gulp*, that many of the teams she played were easy to defeat due to the girls' lack of conditioning, something she knew about personally.

Trait 4

Winners are Coachable

Win-Definition: Coachable—Realizing the value of a coach's input and applying this information to achieve winning status.

Explanation: Dang it! A good coach can be one of an athlete's greatest strengths. Doesn't it seem that so many winning athletes have winning coaches around them? It's not just because the coach is a winning coach, it is because the athlete allows themselves to be coached. Hey, I've seen many an athlete who did not respond to their coach, and the result was usually disastrous. Winning coaches are very, very hard to find, so when an athlete gets one, they need to get on with it and respond to the coaching.

As a side note, why does it always seem that those athletes who had their mom or dad as a coach were winners? I didn't say they were always superstars, but they always seem to have won.

Listen up! If Usain Bolt has coaches and Michael Jordan had coaches.... Need I say more?

Focus Athlete: I can't help but relay this story as it concerns coaching. Going into the 2008 Summer Olympic Games, Jeremy Wariner was as dominant as a winning athlete could be, in any sport. Wariner was the world's best male sprinter in the 400 meters, and we expected him to win the gold medal for the U.S., right? But, something interesting happened along the way.

When arriving in China for the 2008 Games, Wariner had made headlines that he had suddenly changed coaches, and his performances showed that. His association with the legendary Clyde Hart seemed over. In the finals, Wariner was second to LaShawn Merritt of the U.S., a true winner himself. Now, I am not saying that this is the reason that Merritt won or that a silver medal in the Olympics is a losing effort, but it is interesting to ponder.

Since the 2008 Olympics, Wariner reunited with Coach Hart, though he again lost to Merritt at the 2009 World Championships. Had Wariner stayed with Hart through the whole process, would the results have been different? We'll never know, but athletes should take note of this.

Memorable Moment: I heard this story from Bob Rowbotham, the president of *Bigger, Faster, Stronger (BFS)*, a prominent sports performance company since the 1970's. Bob shared about Mark Eaton, a huge, seven-foot-four center for the NBA's Utah Jazz.

Now, big Mark attended UCLA and played sparingly on the basketball team. However, that didn't keep the Jazz from drafting Mark. At that particular time, the Jazz contracted with BFS to train their athletes, and Eaton jumped on board and got going. According to Bob, Eaton was very coachable, eager to improve and help his team win. To summarize this story, Mark Eaton became an NBA all-star and was named the NBA Defensive Player of the Year during his career. Now, how many people have ever won those awards? That's winning. It took a winner like Eaton to be coachable and he helped the Jazz become a winning franchise.

What would have happened if Eaton would have not responded to coaching? Maybe, we would have not attached winner to his name.

"That's Not Winning" Personal Story: I was playing college baseball back in the day, and we had an outfielder who epitomized being "un-coachable." We played for a coach whose teams won on a regular basis. His program was sending players to professional baseball each year it seemed. The years I happened to play, there was a player who would not allow the coaches to get through to him, and it would eventually cost the team

During practice, this player would put on a show when being watched by coaches and scouts, yet paid no attention to the coaches when he was not in the spotlight. The big problem came when we were drilled as right fielders to always back-up throws to first base, in case they were poorly thrown, which he never did. One mark of a winner is to do "winning things" when nobody is watching, but he didn't.

Well, needless to say, we lost a game at state finals because he was nowhere to be found on an overthrown ball to first. He was standing and watching the action, then gave a desperate chase for the ball after realizing his "un-coachability." If he would have just been where the coaches had told him to be, it would have prevented the extra bases for the runners on the other team, who happened to score the winning runs on that day. After the game, he was distraught, yet nobody consoled him, as we all knew what really happened. Because he was uncoachable, the team suffered, and a championship was lost.

Trait 5

Winners are Consistent

Win-Definition: Consistent—Performing winning practices until it becomes automatic behavior.

Explanation: Winners do the same thing over and over and over, and they love it. Do you know why? You already know why, because they are winners. Duh! They make "the routine plays" regularly, and they win. During my training time with athletes, they are required to say, repeatedly I might add, "Repetition equals winning!" I tell them to say like they believe it (whatever). But, it is true. Winning comes from consistent, winning performance, not occasional spectacular performance. Winning may not get you on ESPN's slam dunk highlights, but it will probably get you a tour of the White House because your team won a championship. Boooooo-yahahahaha! Okay, I know there are those who were spectacular winners (Michael Jordan, Tony Hawk, Michael Jordan, Pele, Michael Jordan...), but that isn't the norm. And, besides, does a coach want somebody who does the occasional spectacular (sexy) or one who consistently wins (got a ring, baby!). Teams like the NFL's Pittsburgh Steelers always come to mind when I talk about this "Winners are Consistent" stuff?

Focus Athlete: This athlete is two people with one name, Williams. Tennis's Serena and Venus Williams are the poster children for consistency. If not, then why the heck do you think they're always playing each other for freaking championships? I don't even want to hear about spectacular with them. They're games are so consistently fast, powerful, and calculated that it is the norm for them. Does this make sense? Our spectacular is merely their consistency.

Watch them, I dare you. They do what they do the same way all the time. They put their super abilities to work when they play. They don't hit a couple of gamers then flame out; on the contrary, they hit a bunch of flamers on a regular basis and let the championships continue to roll in. Let's be honest, there have been others in tennis with amazing physical abilities, but they didn't perform with the winning consistency that S and V do (or is it V and S?).

In an interview recently, Venus admitted to the fact that she feels "invincible" on the court. Hello! You want to know why? Venus feels invincible because she plays winning tennis more consistently than others, except for maybe her sister, Serena. It makes perfect sense.

Memorable Moment: I had the pleasure of watching boxing during an incredible era, the 1970's and the 1980's. It was a time for spectacular boxers, as we watched the likes of "Sugar" Ray Leonard, Hector "Macho" Camacho, Ray "Boom Boom" Mancini, and Thomas "The Hit Man" Hearns. During this time, however, was a champion of such consistency, that his record speaks had for itself because he was more consistent than spectacular. He is Larry "The Easton Assassin" Holmes, the heavyweight champion during this time.

It didn't matter whom Holmes faced; he won and they lost. He didn't have an outrageous personality, nor did he live a life that brought a lot of unnecessary attention. He did the most important thing an athlete can do, and that's win. Krikey, the guy won forty-nine straight bouts (listen, that's forty-nine, yo!), twenty-one while defending his title. Now, who does that? Uh, Larry Holmes did that. As I write this, I can't think of too many more athletes who won forty-nine straight anythings, but Larry did. Each and every fight, he consistently executed what he did best, which was better than what his opponents did. You should have gotten that. Winners usually do what they do best better than what their opponents' do best. That was Larry, winning consistently because of consistency (you know that was well said).

"That's Winning" Personal Story: Okay, so there's this girls' soccer team who had a flair for the dramatic, yet a losing record. In three years, this club team had three coaches, until a friend of mine took over. These girls were especially good, several of them legitimate candidates for college scholarships, but their teams lost.

Upon arriving, the coach, much to the disappointment of the girls and their parents (dang parents!), began to corral them by introducing basic soccer skills and strategies. As is usually the case, there was talk of girls quitting and parents running off the coach as they did with the others, but my friend was stalwart, and wouldn't budge (that whole Coach Carter thing). Whenever a player in practice tried a "fancy" play instead of a winning one, she would have to sit out.

As the season began, the team played poorly and lost in the early rounds of their first three tournaments. The coach promised them, however, that the time that they put forth learning to play consistent, winning soccer, would eventually mesh with their advanced abilities, and it did.

All of a sudden, the girls began making the regular plays consistently, and the spectacular followed. They focused on consistency, and the spectacular became regular. They ended up winning some sort of regional cup (that's soccer terms, by the way), and several girls did go onto college to play. The coach told me that after the girls started winning, the only complaints were about the previous years and how they consistently lost. Consistency isn't as sexy as spectacular, but winning is sexier than losing.

Trait 6

Winners are Committed

Win-Definition: Committed—This is who you become by the habits you develop.

Explanation: The commitment I am talking about here isn't the cheapened version used today. What I mean is that commitment just seems to be a word people use but don't really get. The commitment used here is the one that indicates not what you do, but it indicates who you become. Wow! I just said that the commitment winners have is so powerful that it has transformed them from what they do to who they are, which is winners.

Let's revisit the amazing Derek Jeter. In a recent news article, another athlete was quoted as saying that it didn't matter what sport Jeter played, he would just win. And, one of the biggest factors of creating winners is the practices winners have. Did you catch that? Commitment begins at practice. That means that whatever sport Jeter participated in, he would practice until it produced winning, then practice some more. Winning practices determine who you become as an athlete.

Winners are committed to developing their skill sets to the point of what I term as "automatic behavior," and since our behavior defines who we are, winning behavior must lead to the definition of being a winner. They practice and practice until it becomes automatic. They understand that it is practice which wins, not the competition itself. This commitment is what transformed Floyd Mayweather, Jr. from a boxer to a winner, Dara Torres from a swimmer to a winner, and Shaun Johnson from a gymnast to a winner. Can you see this? These athletes perform in their designated sports as others, but they are unlike the others. The others may be competitors or they may be the next-in-liners, but their commitments have not had the impact on them as it has had on the winners I just spoke of. Maybe they are not practicing enough or are practicing the wrong way.

In addition to this, winning athletes are not afraid to see their weaknesses and correct them. This is why they are so committed to developing winning skills, because they realize that it is wise to recognize any weaknesses they may have.

Back in the day of the original bodybuilders (Arnold, Franco, Zane, me, etc.), top pro Bill Grant talked about "priority training". Bill won his share of titles, yet he was always looking at those areas that needed improvement, and improved them. His workouts were his practice, and his commitment to these practices transformed him from a bodybuilder to a winner. He made his weak points a priority during his training time, improved those areas, and proceeded to win some pretty big titles. Committing to recognize weaker areas and improving them says that athletes have a destination to win. Someone who has a goal to win would overlook these and "hope for the best."

Focus Athlete: So, I'm sitting in my personal TV room, the "Black Hole" as my wife calls it (named for the greatest football franchise ever), and on my TV comes a commercial of Tiger Woods. In the commercial, he is shown driving golf balls in the driving rain (sweet!). It's a commercial about commitment, and it indicates that winners are committed to developing their "game," through practice and practice, and more practice. Hey, those who avoid practice have no destination to win. Even Tiger Woods knows that his abilities will only take him so far. Just ask him about his putting. Boy, does he get mad when this isn't going so well, yet his commitment to "winning putting" tells you who he really is. I am sure that putting practice is on his priority practice list.

I watched an interview with "The Tige" (this is what his close friends like me call him, "The Tige" jk) with Michael Wilbon of ESPN. Tiger admitted that he was frustrated when he didn't win.

Bam, baby! He didn't say he was frustrated when he didn't play well or he got frustrated when things didn't go his way. He talks about winning. Chef's talk about food, lawyers talk about law, and winners talk about winning. This is beautiful.

Now, come on, I never think of Tiger Woods practicing. He's Tiger Woods, not some guy trying to make the tour. He doesn't need to practice, right? But, practice he does, and a winner he is. His commitment to developing his winning game sets him apart. Does anybody even look at him as a golfer anymore? I don't know about you, but when I tune in to watch Tiger, I don't tune in to watch golf. I tune in to watch Tiger win. You see? All I know is that when I watch that dude on a Sunday, walking up the course with those black pants and that red shirt, I know what is about to happen.

Note: Though I know Tiger has gone through a pretty bad time in his life lately, I reviewed him here in the book as a winning athlete, and did not take into account his personal issues.

Memorable Moment: This one is going to hurt because it involves my favorite football team, the Oakland Raiders. In the early 2000's, the Raiders were fortunate to have wide receiver Jerry Rice join their team, and he helped them reach the Super Bowl while he was there. He not only was possibly the greatest player to ever play football, he was a winner. Remember. Don't confuse great ability and performance with winning. Winning is the step above greatness and ability.

Rice came to the Raiders with a commitment to developing his skills and a destination to win unlike any other players in the league. When others were doing whatever they did, Rice was perfecting his skills, which is why he won. He would stay behind after the regular practice with coaches or players or anybody who would help and practice some more (catch pass after pass, run route after route). Well, it would seem that when you have someone like Rice on your team, a player who combined greatness and winning, the other players would automatically follow that guy's lead. Unfortunately for the Raiders, the fans, and some players, they did not follow that lead. Now, how dumb is that?

Apparently, the Raiders had a couple of wide receivers who had, *gulp*, potential. Potential is sometimes a code word for "an excuse to lose." Well, instead of hanging around Rice and absorbing everything they possibly could, they did other things. These guys chose to play football on Sundays, not win on Sundays. Did you get that? They were football players, not winners.

As I think about this, why wouldn't these guys stay around to work with Rice? It seems like they could have become winners had they decided to, but they settled for less. I mean, what else were these guys doing after practice that would have been more important than learning to win? Is this making sense? Rice spent so much time perfecting what he did that he went beyond simply winning games. He became a winner. That's the essence of commitment; who you become in the process of what you do, and it begins with practice.

"That's Winning" Personal Story: It was at a local track meet, and my top 800 meter runner, Jared, was set to face a high school superstar runner in the 800 meters. Jared was very good in what he did, but we knew who he was running against. This guy had already blown away the field in an earlier race and was ready to go again.

I looked at Jared and we simultaneously began deciding how we were going to beat him. It was a beautiful moment. We didn't wonder **if** we were going to do this; we decided **how** we were going to do this. That's winning.

It happened as we expected. He ran "on the shoulder" of Jared, thinking he was going to outsprint him with about 200 meters left. We decided to win the race a lot earlier, though. With about ten meters of the first lap left (390 meters), Jared took off. By the time the final 200 meters appeared, he had a fifteen meter lead, and won handily. As you will see, Jared had that race won before the day of the event.

Jared was committed to his training, as he would train on his own at times and just tell me what he was doing. He had that stupid hill behind his house and always wanted to get away from the track to do what I call "terrain train." He had a destination to win, and he did. His commitment was really a transformation, from gifted runner to winner. Before his high school career was over, he was the league champion for three consecutive years in the 800 meters and the 300 meter hurdles. You know the funny thing? He told me this would happen after his freshman year, and you know what, I didn't doubt him a bit. He decided to win for three years, and his commitment to developing his skill "sealed the deal."

Oh, that runner Jared beat was Ryan Hall from Big Bear High School, who is the number one marathon runner for the U.S. at this time.

Trait 7

Winners are Confident

Win-Explanation: Confident—Performing without doubt or fear.

Explanation: To quote the legendary NFL football coach Vince Lombardi, upon questioning about his Green Bay Packers losing a game, Lombardi said, "The Packers don't lose, they just run out of time." That's confidence, knowing that somehow, someway, you will win, and the Packers did, again and again. Winners know that there are all kinds of ways to win. Outlast your opponent, pummel you opponent, wear down your opponent, and on and on and on. Winners just know they will win. Confidence is not trying to figure out how to avoid losing, but rather, it is deciding a way to win. It is not, "if I will win," it is "how I will win."

This is why I say that winners have a destination to win, not a goal or a dream. With a goal or dream to win, an athlete can doubt if they will win, and yet justify it by saying, "I tried my best" or "I left it on the field." It all sounds fine and good, but they lost. And, I'm okay with that. This book is why winners win. It is not an attack on those who don't. But, I am sure that are many who will read this and decide that they deserve to win and that they are going to start doing so, changing from goals and dreams to destinations. Yoooo Hooooo!

I mean, I don't think snowboarder Shaun White ever even considers losing. I am pretty sure that he is too busy deciding how he is going to win, and he does, with amazing consistency. I remember watching Laila Ali box, and there was no doubt in my mind or hers that she would win. I am not saying that winning won't be a struggle. I'm just saying that winners are confident that they will find a way to win.

Focus Athlete: Though neither of these ladies is actively playing right now, I am going to talk about two women who are absolute crack-ups. I say crack-ups because when they appear, it's already game over. You don't think that freaks out their opponents? What an advantage. They come to the playing area knowing they will win (without arrogance) when their opponent is thinking the same thing. Awesome!

The world of women's beach volleyball has been completely dominated by Misty May and Kerri Walsh. Man, when they walked onto the sand, whether it was in Huntington Beach, CA or Beijing, China, it was just understood that they would win, and they knew that, too. Their confidence, not cockiness, is evident by how they carry themselves. They were completely into winning and cared less about the things going on around them. They didn't give a rip if they "won big" or just "got by". If they had to adjust their game during the match, they did. Style was not their destination, winning was.

Have you ever watched an athlete who had no confidence? It is terrifying. With no confidence, the things that they normally do don't work anymore. They hit weak groundballs, their serves go out of bounds or into the nets, tee shots end up off of the fairway, or their flips on a four-inch beam are hesitant and potentially dangerous. Once an athlete's confidence ebbs, negative things begin to happen.

To Misty and Kerri, their confidence is more like faith to them. These two women, like all winning athletes, know that when they do the things they are supposed to do, it becomes winning, and, like we talked about before, they become winners. Look up the word *confident* in a dictionary. The definition given may say, *Misty May and Kerri Walsh.*

Memorable Moment: So, I'm watching this world championship track and field meet several years ago, and something unbelievable happens, right on TV.

As the camera spanned the competition area, it was clear that tension was running high. Heck, it was the world championships. Players were jumping around, walking around and yelling at nothing, and breathing pretty hard. I guess they were nervous about the possibility of losing (ooh, good one). And, then, all of a sudden, there she was, Yelena Isinbayeva.

Russia's Yelena Isinbayeva is the world's greatest, winningest women's pole vaulter, and the camera caught her preparing for her tension-filled, endorphine-releasing pole vault competition. She was lying on the ground sleeping with a towel over her head so that nobody would bother her. Can you believe it? Everybody else around her is totally amped up, but she's sleeping! Not only was she sleeping, she had told the pole vault judges to skip her turns until the bar was raised to a height where she would win. Hey, it's the pole vault, where athletes are in the air, seventeen plus feet off of the ground, armed only with a plastic pole and a distant mat below them. This isn't chess, brother. Now, either Isinbayeva was supernaturally confident or she has one of those sleep disorders. If I'm not mistaken, she set a new world record that day. It seemed that the outcome had already been decided and all the other competitors were merely competing to see who was going to finish second that day.

In all of my years of watching winners win, I can't remember any of them sleeping before their game, match, or competition began. Not Edwin Moses, not Peyton Manning, not Mia Hamm, and not even Mike Tyson, a man who routinely destroyed his opponents early in his boxing career. I mean, how do you even respond to that? Crazy.

"That's Winning" Personal Story: One of the most enjoyable moments of my coaching career came the first year I coached a girls' high school varsity basketball team. These girls were winners. They didn't win a championship, but they were winners.

In one particular game, it was very close and we were down to four girls due to fouls. Four girls! Well, as the other team began catching up, we were confident we would win the game, somehow, someway.

With about thirty seconds left, the other team came within one point. During a time out, one of my players, Jen, told the team that she would handle the ball, draw a foul, and make two free throws to win the game. I was stunned. This was not her personality, or so I thought. Her confidence level was so high that I didn't bother saying anything, except, "Okay."

Just as she planned, the other team decided to foul her with about twenty seconds left, and I'll be darned if she didn't make two free throws. The game ended positively for us. With only four girls on the floor, we harassed the other team who finally made a basket with only a few seconds left, leaving us one point ahead. This same girl took the inbounds pass and sprinted down the floor before the other team could foul her, thus winning the game.

When I asked her about this later on, she merely told me that she was sure that we would win and that she wasn't really scared at any time. Confidence is a beautiful thing, and winners wear it well.

Trait 8

Winners are Courageous

Win-Explanation: Courageous—Those who "step up" when needed most.

Explanation: Winners do not fear losing. That's what makes them winners. Winners don't freak out during close games and don't get uptight if it's a close battle. Most of all, they don't fear the "big shot" or the "winning play." I really believe that the game is never "on the line" to them. Because they are winners, whether the game is close or a blow-out, they don't seem to differentiate between the two. It's almost like practice to them, no big deal. Do you know why winners want the critical moment in the game to be focused on them? It's because, to them, it's not a critical moment, it's just the game, which they usually find a way to win anyway. Does that make sense?

I use the word courageous because that is what it seems like to us; like having the courage to be at the plate when the game is in question, or needing a winning performance on the Olympic rings when the teams need it the most. To them, this is what they do. They would perform the same way if the game in on the line or not. It is we who make up these big moments, not the winners. They are already prepared to win, no matter what part of the game it is or what part of the season it is.

Heck, I grew up watching baseball's "Mr. October," Reggie Jackson, who routinely came through in the playoffs and World Series with legendary winning performances. To him, it was just baseball, and because he was a winner, it looked courageous. I really do not think that Reggie thought, coming up to bat at a critical time, "Oooh, the pressure's on. I'd better be courageous and do something." I think Reggie understood situations, but as a winner, he was going to perform automatically.

Focus Athlete: Out here on the West Coast, we have a courageous winner named "D Fish," who plays for the NBA'S Los Angeles Lakers. Derek Fisher, without question, is a winner. He has never been identified as a superstar, but his status as a winner is well-known and well respected. I guarantee you. Any coach in the NBA would love to have Fisher on his team. The courage of "D Fish" should be explained this way.

Over the years, the Lakers have needed a "big shot" in a game for whatever reason, and Fisher was seemingly always there to deliver (get it? D Liver, D Fish?). One of his shots against the San Antonio Spurs was so courageous, that they nicknamed it the "Fish Swish." That's hysterical. Over and over in his career, Fisher just comes up with these shots. We just witnessed it as the Lakers beat the Orlando Magic for the 2009 NBA title. Fisher just kinda came up with a game-tying shot when the Lakers needed it. Now for us, the fans, it was courageous. For Fisher, it's just what winners do. I'm telling you, game on the line or not, he would have made it. D Fish understands the moments of the game, but to him, those are shots he's supposed to make because that's what winners do. At no point did Fisher ever consider the fact that he would miss those shots. If he did, so what? He's not afraid to lose, and he's always ready to win.

A talented or gifted player would not do this like Fisher does. An athlete whose goal is to win or who hopes to win won't make these shots. That's what separates D Fish from the others. His destination is to win, and when he performs in the "big moment," that's who he is. Literally, he is "The Fish Who Saved L.A.," more than once, I might add.

Hey, winners don't fear the big moments. They're so focused on winning, the "big moments" don't register with them; it's just another play.

Memorable Moment: In the late 70's, early 80's, there were some pretty competitive moments between the Kansas City Royals and the New York Yankees in major league baseball. It was during a playoff game that I remember one of sports' most courageous moments.

In this particular game, the Royals were trailing the Yankees, and were running out of time. Fortunately for the Royals, they had a player named George Brett, who was all about winning. In this instance, George Brett came to bat with runners on the bases, and something needed to happen for them. Just at the right time, Brett jacks a homer to win the game. It was amazing, something only winners do.

It was after the game, when they interviewed Brett, did this concept of courageous come to me. His comments were even greater than the home run itself. Now remember, courageous is the term that I use to describe this particular trait of winning. Brett really didn't do anything courageous; he was just being "Brett the Winner."

To get to the point, when asked, Brett said something that only a winner would say. The reporter asked him about the importance of the home run, and Brett's response floored me. Brett said that when he came to bat, he realized that the Royals needed a home run, so he hit one. Huh? Now, how often does that happen? We needed a home run, so I hit one? Un-freaking-believable. Now, to me, that's totally courageous. But, to Brett, that is just what he did.

Winners don't get all tweaked-out about so-called big, or important situations. They just perform the way they are supposed to perform, and they win. If that hitter wasn't Brett, I think that maybe he wouldn't be up there deciding to hit a home run. On the contrary, he may have been up to bat hoping not to mess it up. Winners deliver in the "big" moments without a second thought, whereas most others are hoping that they don't mess things up. Huge difference, huh?

"That's Winning" Personal Story: I have a friend who pitches in the major leagues at this time. He decided he was going to get there, and he did. That's winning.

Before the major leagues, he became committed to this destination by staying afterwards when everyone else went home. He was already one of the top players, not only on his team, but in the entire region. His commitment was so strong, the coach gave him the keys to the baseball facilities and told him to make sure he locked up. This way, he could stay as long as he needed to in order to become a major leaguer.

So many just dream of the majors, yet do not understand the winner you must become to get there. This kid did, and, hopefully, he remembered to give the keys back to the coach.

Trait 9

Winners are Calculators

Win-Definition: Calculators—Those who figure out how to defeat the opposition.

Explanation: Winners have a knack for figuring out how to win games, races, or competitions. They are so good at what they do that they can actually form a strategy as to how to beat their opponents. They can evaluate the situation or competition and come up with a plan to be victorious.

You see this all of the time. It may be Rafael Nadal calculating how to beat Roger Federer in tennis, which he did with regularity. It might have been one of those dang Kenyan runners who would seemingly always upset world record holder Hicham El Guerrouj in the Olympic 1500 meters. Heck, in his prime, Oakland Raider Hall of Famer Howie Long, in order to win, used to talk about how he would bulk-up or slim down, depending on his upcoming competition. In my thoughts, most people just do the best they can and hope for the best. Not winners, they know what they are doing and execute it with winning results.

Focus Athletes: I just finished watching the women's volleyball team from Penn State University win their third consecutive NCAA championship. Third? Really? Their opponent, the University of Texas, played winning volleyball that day. They had Penn State down two games to zero, and were ready to take the title back home to Austin. For Penn State, something had to be done to regain control of the match, and they did.

Coming into the third, and possibly final game, Penn State coach Russ Rose and players, including All-American Megan Hodge, decided on a strategy they needed to overcome the deficit and put it into action. They were able to calculate what it took to win the championship, and did.

Whatever adjustments Penn State made were those that were needed. Texas, led by Destinee Hooker's epic effort, was in control early in the match. In short, whatever the Penn Staters did to adjust was more effective than what Texas did. Penn State made a winning calculation that day, and championship number three is now history.

What Penn State was able to accomplish was no different from what winning teams do all over the country, at all levels. Whether it's women's basketball at the University of Connecticut, men's basketball at Duke University, lacrosse at Syracuse University, women's soccer at North Carolina University, or football at De La Salle High School in Concord, California, winners calculate how to use their abilities in order to win. They may not have "the most talent" at all times, but they calculate what it takes to win and do year after year after year.

Surfing great Kelly Slater calculates how to win a surf tournament and Dianna Taurasi calculates how to drive past her WNBA opponents, and they're winners, so...

Memorable Moment: It was 1974 in the African nation of Kenya, and legendary boxer Muhammed Ali, was fighting the reigning heavyweight champion, George Foreman (yes, the Lean, Mean Grilling Machine guy). It was termed "The Rumble in the Jungle". Foreman was a fan favorite because he had won a gold medal in the 1972 Olympics in Munich, Germany at only nineteen years old.

Foreman came into the match heavily favored to win because his punches were too powerful for his opponents. But, Ali, being the winner that he was, had already calculated as to how to beat Foreman that night. Ali fully unveiled his boxing strategy called the "Rope-a-Dope". This strategy allowed Foreman to punch away at Ali while Ali covered up to absorb the punches harmlessly. By the ninth round, Foreman was done and Ali proceeded to knock him out to win the heavyweight title. He simply calculated his way to a win, much to the surprise of millions of boxing fans.

"That's Winning" Personal Story: When I coached cross country, we attended an amazing event each year at Mt. San Antonio College (Mt. SAC) in Southern California. Hundreds of kids ran each race, all hoping to finish in the top nine in their heat. The top nine got a medal, and the runners proudly wore them throughout the day for all to see.

My top boy runner, Irvin, told me that year that he was going to finish in the top nine, but I had my doubts. Well, as the race went on, he was in thirty-third place when he headed up a brutal hill called the "switchbacks". As history will show, my guy came down the "switchbacks" in seventh place. I was flabbergasted and started yelling at him telling him he had cheated (nice coaching, huh?). Wisely, he continued to the finish line and placed seventh to win a medal.

When I got to him, instead of congratulating him, I began to question what he did. He instantly told me that all he did was follow his plan to win, which was to pass the other runners on the "switchbacks". He told me that many of the other runners walked up the hill, and some even sat. He reminded me that I taught all of our runners to say, "Hills are my friend" and that's where many races could be won (by then, I was feeling even more stupid). He knew before the race that this was his plan, and it worked. Good thing he got it, because I certainly didn't.

Trait 10

Winners are Converters

Win-Definition: Converters—They do what they do well better than what their opponents do.

Explanation: How in the world some athletes win the ways that they do is completely unfathomable to me. I mean, I see less physically talented players consistently win over those who seem to be much more superior athletically. It appears that no matter how it looks or how it seems, they just win. These guys are not always the fastest or the strongest, but they win. They have found a way to do what they do better than their opponents do what they do. Then again, there are those athletes who have phenomenal skills who win. The point is this. Winners use their talent, a lot or not, and convert it into winning performance.

As an example, there are quarterbacks in the NFL who have the absolute look of a winner. They have great footwork, their ball spirals, they are well-built, etc., etc., etc. Then, you see a guy like Phillip Rivers of the San Diego Chargers, whose throwing motion is the most ungodly thing I've ever seen, but he wins. When he has to scramble away from defenders, it doesn't look so good, but he's a winner. He converts his abilities into winning. He takes whatever it is he can do and figures out to use it to win.

It comes down to looking good at what you do, which guarantees nothing, or using the skills that you have to win something.

Focus Athlete: OK, so I'm watching this quarterback with blood all over his face out on the field yelling something to somebody, all fired up. Now, the blood thing was from a small cut on his nose or forehead or something. It looked cool for the TV audience, but that's not the point. This guy is the perfect example of someone who uses whatever skill he might have to win. His name is Tim Tebow, the Heisman Trophy winning quarterback for the University of Florida.

I do not think there is anything that Tebow does that looks good when he does it, but he wins. His throwing motion doesn't seem to inspire anybody, but he wins. He looks anything but athletic when he runs, but he wins. But, but, but he wins. He is able to convert whatever he can do into winning. He doesn't care how it looks or if it gets shown on the TV highlights after the game. He is a winner, and this cannot be disputed. So, when too many others are trying to get their faces on TV or show up another player, Tebow is winning. By combining Tebow's winning nature with his ability to convert his skills to win, it's no wonder that his team won two national championships in three years.

Memorable Moment: There is only one story which fits here. This is the story of the 1980 U.S. Olympic hockey team, immortalized in the movie *Miracle.*

It was 1980, and our country was going through some rough times. In the meantime, coach Herb Brooks, a legendary college hockey coach was busy assembling a hockey team for the Olympics, but things were not going well. Standing in the way of everybody was the hockey team from the Soviet Union, which has now separated into about fifteen different countries I think. The Russians were so good, and so dominate, that they would play the best professional players from the National Hockey League (NHL), and beat them. What kind of chance did these players have? They were amateurs from the college ranks, not professionals like the Russians or NHL players were. Right before the Olympics started, the Russians had pummeled the U.S. team 9-0. It was not a pretty thing.

Then, history was made. The American team began getting what Coach Brooks was teaching them (coachable, baby!) and wins were happening. Suddenly, on TV around the world, the Americans defeated the Russians, and went on to beat the Swedish team to win the gold medal. It was near the end of the U.S. and Russia game when sportscaster Al Michaels proclaimed, "Do you believe in miracles?" Miracle? Maybe. But, upon further review, the U.S. players finally converted all of the teaching, coaching, and talent they had into one of the most memorable wins in sports history. U.S. players Ken Morrow, Mike Eruzione, and others translated this accomplishment into winning careers in the NHL and in business. It's amazing what winning does for a person.

"That's Winning" Personal Story: OK, another cross country story. I had the pleasure of coaching a really talented runner on the Jr. High level, who was a winning runner for my teams until her knees told her to quit. Kendall not only ran well, but she learned at a young age what it took to win.

We arrived at the league finals and Kendall knew that she had to keep her number three overall position in order to give our team a chance to place as a team. This would be the first time our school had placed in the top three teams, so we were all excited. As she passed me on her first mile, she yelled to me that she was feeling sick, and I just became immediately depressed. I didn't know until after the race that she had eaten an orange right before she started running.

So, as I waited near the finish line, hoping, hoping, hoping, here she came, clearly in third place. I noticed as she was running, she was turning her head to the left every ten yards or so. As she was running, she was totally throwing up this orange she had eaten, but refused to stop. It was truly unbelievable. I wanted to tell her to stop, but I knew she had decided to finish in third that day, and throwing up or not, she did. She threw up as she passed me and headed right for the finish chute. About a minute later, I heard a voice over the course P.A. system announce, "Attention all coaches. Please tell your athletes to refrain from throwing up on the scorer's table." I couldn't help but laugh. Let's face it. She decided to win that day, and she did. Our team finished third overall, and bringing that trophy home that day was a thing of beauty.

Bonus Trait

Winners are Coveted

Win-Definition: Coveted—Those players who coaches want.

Explanation: All coaches want to win. The smart ones, however, place a value on players who win, not just on players who have talent or who are gifted. Thus, if a player has learned to win, and have become a winner in the process, they will be coveted by winning coaches who have winning programs (whew, that's a lot of winning!).

I remember when men's basketball coach Ben Howland took over the head coaching position at the University of California Los Angeles (UCLA), and he talked about his recruiting efforts. Howland came to UCLA after several of the top players had committed to other colleges and universities. Thus, Howland stated that he concentrated his efforts pursuing players who were talented, yet came from winning programs. Howland was able to recruit winners such as Jordan Farmar, Arron Afflalo, Kevin Love, and Darren Collison. These players were all winners who were able to take their careers to the NBA.

Howland, one of the best coaches in the nation, covets players who are winners. For those who apply the *10 Traits* to their games, they will be sure to be coveted by coaches at the next level. Coaches know that it takes more than talent to win. It takes players who have become winners to win. Coaches are pretty smart.

Focus Athlete: As I write this book, probably the most coveted player in the NBA is about to become a free agent, which gives every team in professional basketball a chance to sign him for their team. He's coveted by teams and by corporations, especially the Nike Corporation. That's what winning does. That player is LeBron James. Teams are already making salary cap room in order to present him with an offer. These teams do not covet LeBron for his skills, but rather for his ability to win. You see, whatever team LeBron ends up with, that team will automatically have a chance to win the NBA title. In short, that makes him coveted.

It has been a pleasure to watch LeBron transform from a great player to a winner. He is not into personal accomplishments anymore. His heart is set on winning, winning, then winning some more. Did you read that? His heart is set on winning, not his mind. He no longer has a goal or a dream; he has a destination to win, especially after having watched Kobe Bryant and the Lakers win it all in 2009. This is why the Cleveland Cavaliers, LeBron's current team brought in Shaquille O'Neal. They brought in this winner to help LeBron win. It's not about fame and fortune now, it's about winning.

Winners are coveted. The best thing about winning is that everyone can win at their particular level. Teams want to win, thus they are looking for winners. By applying the traits listed in this book, you **will** become the winner that a team or company or a business is looking for. I know winning isn't easy, but it is worth it. Heck, in five years, you're going to be five years older anyway. You may as well learn to win, so that in five years, you have reached your destination while the others are still setting goals and having dreams.

Memorable Moment: I will tell you about one of the greatest winners in NBA history that I witnessed play out his career. He is a guy that only true basketball fans and true students of winning (you know, like me) understand. The coaches he played for and players he played with, they knew he was a winner. His name is Ron Harper, one of the great winners in recent basketball history.

Ron Harper came to the NBA as a great player. He purposely (purposely, yo, purposely!) adjusted his game in order to lead his teams to wins. Ron Harper had the ability to lead the NBA in scoring in any given year, yet that was not his focus. Ron chose to win and to captain others to win, even at the risk of lesser statistics. Let me put it this way. Throughout his career, when a team in the NBA was at the point of winning, but needed that certain player, these teams would go out and get Ron Harper. Being a winner, he was coveted by those who coveted winning. Just ask the Chicago Bulls and the Los Angeles Lakers about Ron Harper. They will tell you the same thing. Harper was instrumental in helping both of these franchises win NBA championships.

Winners are coveted. People want to be associated with winners, and there is a great deal of reward that comes along with winning. Ron Harper could have easily fallen into the trap of being successful or achieving greatness. However, he won, which is always greater than success or greatness.

"That's Winning" Personal Story: I used to announce the football games at one of the schools that I worked at, which leads me to this story.

In this particular year, the school's football team had the ability to win their league title (and some playoff games) in a very competitive division. The coach was a winner by his actions, integrity, and his coaching style. The players were great kids who were learning how to win. Previously, the school had some pretty lame efforts and behavior on the field, thus this team was refreshing.

In the season's biggest game, a winning moment occurred. The team had just scored a touchdown, but was one point behind. They did not want to tie the game and have to play overtime, so they decided to win the game (exciting, huh?). Well, one of the team captains (of course!), Rusty, just kinda decided that he would score a two-point conversion to win the game. Now, how do you just kinda decide to do that?

So, as I announced that the teams were coming to the line of scrimmage, the whole place was going beserk. Rusty took the handoff from the quarterback and drove towards the goal line, where he was met forcefully by a couple of defenders. To end the suspense, he kept driving and driving until he got into the end zone for the two points they needed to win the game, and eventually, the league title. You can't say that "he wanted it more" (I hate that stupid saying), because that may not be true. Who knows how badly the other team wanted that win? No, this captain, he decided to instead of wanting to. Deciding to and wanting to separate wins and losses, don't you agree?

On the following Monday, when I saw Rusty on campus, I asked him about that play. He told me, very humbly and matter-of-factly, that he needed to score those points, so he did. I still see him in our community these days, and the winner that he was on the field has continued by the winning business man and person he still is.